Marc Glorius
Jale Maria Gönenc

hommage - to pioneers

a two days conversation with
David B. Sutcliffe

Bibliografische Informationen der Deutschen Nationalbibliothek:
Die Deutsche Nationalbibliothek verzeichnet diese Publikation
in der deutschen Nationalbibliografie; detaillierte bibliografische
Daten sind im Internet über http://dnb.dnb.de abrufbar

Buchgestaltung: Martin Haeusler

© 2020 Marc Glorius

Herstellung und Verlag: BoD – Books on Demand, Norderstedt

ISBN: 9783751948050

Preface

This booklet is gathering a long two days discussion Jale and me had with David B. Sutcliffe in january 2015 and an essay on him, his schools, Kurt Hahn and the idea in general.

This work was done in order to transmit and explore first hand David B. Sutcliffe's legacy.

Read well!

Jale Maria Gönenc
Marc Glorius

Content

Interview	9
Sutcliffe about Sutcliffe	9
Sutcliffe about Kurt Hahn	16
Sutcliffe about education / Europe / international schools	30
Pioneers - Marc Glorius	43
David Brook Sutcliffe (1934-2019)	45
Boarding schools in „strong places" ...	45
... based on old principles	47
Raising the barriers, opening the walls, „décloisonnement"	49
Intensa internazionale e mondiale	50
Kurt Hahn	51
Sutcliffe: an idiosycratic founder and creative figure	55

Interview

We met in January 2015 in London Pimlico. David and Elisabeth Sutcliffe welcomed us warmly in their apartment. It was a mild, sunny January day. After a short lunch, we went to the salon for a conversation lasting several hours. There were four of us: David (DS), his wife Elisabeth (ES), Jale (JG) and me (MG). Elisabeth took part only occasionally. The next day we met David at the Grosvenor Hotel at Victoria Station.

Sutcliffe about Sutcliffe

MG: Suppose you live to be 160 years old. What would you do?
DS and ES laugh.
DS: I have to finish writing this book about Hahn. It has become something of a burden. A biography. It should have been published 30 years ago.

JG: What's so burdensome about it?
DS: A lot of work. Especially the political side. I mean, he had so many contacts, even after he had „retired". Letters of a whole year, an enormous mass ...

ES: The family asked him to write it.
DS: That's my main occupation, my main job. And Mostar is still a lot of work. We have to raise money. It's not that easy anymore.

JG: What else would you like to learn?
DS: History ... If I can, I read historical books. I am currently reading a book about Napoleon's campaign in Russia: fascinating and cruel.

MG: Is it true that you crossed the Atlantic to America by sailboat?
DS: Yes, that's right.

MG: In the sense of an expedition – Kurt Hahn?
DS: Yes.

MG: How long did it take you?
DS: 43 days.

MG: Did you always want to be a schoolteacher?
DS: No. The only thing I did not want to do was become a teacher. When you have to decide what you want to do when you are 18 or 20, it is very understandable that you do not want to become a teacher. Because you have had enough of teachers. You cannot imagine that being a teacher can be a nice job. I had studied languages in Cambridge, German and French. Spent a year in France, in Brittany.
I had been to Germany once, for 20 days, but I knew little German.
I did my exams, not very well, but I did them after all. Then I decided to go to Germany. Six months, I thought, to improve

my German etc. Then I wanted to do military service, even though I grew up on the island of Guernsey where they had no compulsory military service there. It only existed for England. I knew that if I wanted to work in England, I had to do military service beforehand. In Germany I had a friend – an Englishman – who was a teacher in Salem. He was primarily a mentor, an international boarding school mentor.

When I arrived at the family in Karlsruhe, where I had been for 20 days earlier, there was a letter from him. In the letter he asked me if I wanted to come to Salem. He had decided to go back to England. His job was good, as he said. So I went there, got the job for a year. In the meantime, compulsory military service in England was gradually abolished and I still didn't know what to do with my life. I stayed in Salem for almost four years. I met Elisabeth, my wife, in my last year there.

And it was in Salem where I met Kurt Hahn. He liked everything about England. He was an „anglophile", as they say. The English students who came to Salem used to have breakfast or dinner with him or played tennis. I got to know Hahn well. And was extremely impressed by him at the time. He told me about Atlantic College. That was when he was preparing and organising Atlantic College. He then financially helped me to visit all his Outward Bound Schools in Scotland and England.

I did that during the summer. Finally, I left Salem at Easter 1960 and had six months off. I worked as his private secretary in London. It wasn't a lot of work. I mean, I walked around a bit seeing a lot of people. Then I got to go Gordonstoun for a year. That year I was offered a job at Atlantic College. I went there.

I later became a headmaster. I was the second headmaster of Atlantic College and the first in Duino. It is easier to be the first.

You make a lot of mistakes and they will always be forgiven, since you are just in a trial phase etc. The successes are credited and the failures are forgiven. The second headmaster can no longer rely on that. This development seems to be a general rule. It's much more fun to be a founder, also for the students. Even in Mostar: at first we thought we would open the college in a suburb of Sarajevo. This was not possible for various reasons.

We were thinking of a smaller college with 100 students; we thought we would take all the hundred students. They would stay there for two years, then leave. Then we would take another hundred. The idea was that all students felt like foreverunders. Every generation would have been a founding generation. We had never been able to start this experiment.

A pity actually. It would have been an interesting project. The best qualities emerge when you break new ground.

MG: What was your best experience?
DS: I don't know. A very important experience: I was at the Hungarian border for three weeks at Christmas 1956, where the refugees crossed the border after the Budapest uprising. It was very cold, there was snow and they came over. We found that many came in one night. The next night hardly anyone. Then we found out: They came from inland by train. This train arrived at 1:00 a.m. Near the border. They all got out. The train driver always made a sound with the siren, so we heard that they were coming. These refugees were dependent on guides to lead them across the border. Of course, these were paid. One night they took the money from the refugees and led them across the border. The next night, they took the police money and handed them the refugees. The first night someone came who had his calf shot from the foot. Yes gone. That was a bit adventurous. When the uprising began in

Budapest, I happened to be lying in bed with a fever and listened to the radio all the time, listened to all the programs.

MG: Where were you then?
DS: In Salem. I heard the broadcasts: „Help us!" It was very dramatic. During the Christmas holidays, I was at the border. After a few days you got a little tired, not having slept all night. There was someone who told me: when you go to Vienna you have to sleep in your apartment and get a good rest. On Christmas Eve I went there, went to bed, slept. When I woke up it was already a day after Christmas. So I have one Christmas less than I am old. The then headmaster of Salem, Prince Georg Wilhelm of Hanover, offered to take in 80 Hungarian youngsters. Of course free of charge. That's how it was done. And they graduated from high school there.

MG: Did you experience the war personally?
DS: Indirectly. We lived on the island of Guernsey, a Channel Island. Nobody expected Hitler to suddenly come over all of Europe. So when he started marching through, it dawned on the people of the Channel Islands and also in London that the Channel Islands would be occupied. They are very close to France. Suddenly the panic started: in ten days, half of the population was evacuated. About 45,000 people were embarked and taken to England.
My father was a doctor, a general practitioner. We had only come to Guernsey from England in 1936 and bought ourselves into a practice. The health system was private at the time and his older colleague, Montegory, was a Jew. When the Germans got closer it was clear that he had to leave with his family in any case. And he did leave. It was said that my father would definitely have to stay.

Who else should take care of the patients? At the very last moment we went over to England, because it was of course difficult to get a place on the ships. You also had to use your elbows. At the last moment we got the seats. We, that is my mother, my two siblings and me. There were four of us. I still remember exactly how I went to bed – I was five years old. I slept and then we were woken up and at 10:00 in the evening we were on the ship. I experienced the war from England, as a refugee.

MG: Where did you find accommodation? Were there families who took in evacuees?
DS: Of course my mother had to make ends meet. Montegory had lent her £ 200 to take care of the family. We went to my grandparents first. Then we stayed for a while in a house that belonged to my uncle. We stayed with different families.

ES: But always in private homes.
DS: Always private. In June 1945 we came back to Guernsey.

JG: Did your father stay on Guernsey all the time?
DS: Yes, he stayed there during the occupation. As a result, he was of course not very friendly-minded towards the Germans.
ES: I was in Hamburg at the beginning of the war and was evacuated against the English. I am from Hamburg.

MG: Where were you evacuated to?
PS: To Swabia. Initially near Schwäbisch Gmünd. Later – my father was appointed to the university in 1942 – to Tübingen.

JG: It is interesting that a German-English connection was created regarding the circumstances.

DS: Yes. Her family has some English blood.

ES: My mother corresponded with her English relatives during the war via the Red Cross in Geneva. Once a month she was allowed to write a letter with just a few words – 30 words or so. Just to let them know: we're fine and how are you?

DS: My parents were officially allowed to exchange 25 words a month, also by telegrams via the Red Cross. Then my father somehow found out: There was no limit to sending letters to English prisoners of war in Germany. They were then allowed to exchange letters with their relatives in England. So he then wrote his letters to Germany, which were then copied and then again. …. Others have suffered more from the war than we have. But it was war. I also saw some bombs in London.

JG: Basically, this is what happens to people coming here today, too. I mean people who come from a war and suddenly have to find somewhere else to stay with other people. It is a similar moment. When you need support: either family or some other form of community who helps you get a foothold and live on. I think it's important to hear that again today. What happens does not only happen now, it already happened to our parents. It is important to call this into awareness.

MG: A maternal great uncle of mine was one of the first colored generals in France. When I was little, my mother said to me at a family reunion: ask uncle Tonton Hector what the war was like. I then asked. He just replied: uninteresting and terrible. I didn't talk to him much anyway. But I remember this: war is terrible, keep your hands off it. That was the only message I got from this great uncle.

ES: A general.

MG: Yes. He has experienced a lot, his plane was shot down by Germans over Holland, he was the only survivor ... But he said with a look that I remember, sad and loving: „Forget the war. Better worry about peace."
My mother is French, my father German, mixed. Similar to Jale: German-Turkish. First generation. Where a family did not come to the wedding: you do not marry a German.
ES/DS: It was the same with us.

JG: It was the same with my parents.

Sutcliffe about Kurt Hahn

JG: How would you see Kurt Hahn's spirit of experiential education today? Does it still exist? How could you transfer it to your work?

DS: Hahn wanted the Atlantic College in Wales. And it wouldn't have been founded without him. That is clear. His basic idea at the beginning of the 1960s: Cuban missile crisis, east-west conflict, nuclear weapons. His first idea was to strengthen the so-called Atlantic community. Germans, French, English and Americans, NATO member states should create a cultural community really well. The youth of these countries was to be healthy and idealistic, etc. They should want freedom and other good things. And work for it. In a second step, students from other countries were then accepted. He thought in particular of pupils from the communist countries, the former „Eastern Bloc". Hahns's grandmother was Polish. He had a certain relationship with Poland. He said, rightly so, that there are so many young people in Poland looking west. You should let them participate. They may have the same ideals, but they are not allowed to pursue them because of the political circumstances. It was somewhat successful to bring young people from Eastern Europe to the colleges. Of course, on a small scale, but it worked. Incidentally, there were already German students at Atlantic College back in 1962, which is overlooked today. Right at the beginning. They weren't very welcome in Wales at the time. But then everything went very well. A few years later, the first Poles came to college. Then in the 1970s several students from Poland and Yugoslavia. In the 1970s, the first Chinese came, one Russian and a Russian teacher came, thanks to Mountbatten. Well, small but important successes. Atlantic College was the first school to accept Chinese students after the Cultural Revolution. They came in a group. They were 12 – all paid for by the Chinese government. There were great people. When the college in Italy opened in 1982, we put a lot of emphasis on East-West communication. We had students from all over the Eastern Bloc, including Belarus. When the Berlin Wall fell, a third of the school was Eastern European. It was quite a success.

The college in Mostar is a continuation of this idea: a school – not to be founded in Germany, England or Italy – but in a country that had recently seen war itself and where the divisions between the different parts of the population are still very much alive. For that reason: Mostar. I believe the United World Colleges should still find groundbreaking ways today.

JG: Does that mean that it is in the spirit of Kurt Hahn to always initiate something new?
DS: Yes. He was very politically active in the First World War and close to the top people. Especially as the main advisor to Prince

Max von Baden in the last weeks of the war. In the end, of course, that didn't go very well. But who could have taken responsibility for Germany in October 1918? Who would have been successful? I mean it was a hopeless situation. Completely hopeless. And Max bore the responsibility for this, with his colleagues and with Hahn. And then he was fiercely criticised for it and for everything that happened there.

Hahn said that during the war he had seen with his own eyes how leading people had not had the courage to live their convictions. Although they had been very intelligent, but too weak in character to make important decisions and take important initiatives.

Hahn also said that they had not had the courage to negotiate with the enemy on a real basis. That is why he claims in his educational approach that everything depends on character. Education must form character in such a way that a person develops the courage to stand up for what is „recognised as correct". No matter what the others say. Whether others laugh at it or whether they are against it. One has to follow one's conscience. How can you make sure that a person not only talks but acts? Acts according to his conscience. And to make his point convincingly. Because conscience is an unstable matter. There is an example: a doctor is woken up at night by a patient calling. The doctor has the opportunity to ask certain questions. Questions that encourage reassuring answers. Or you can ask other questions that really come to the point. That is why the doctor must have good character. He really has to take care of the patient. And he shouldn't ask questions that allow him to stay in bed. What could be the right questions?

So how can you make sure that a person – gifted, intelligent, educated – is able to follow his conscience? In his youth, he must have certain experiences that strengthen him for the future. He must be able to think back on something. He must have a stronger will when remembering these experiences. The will to enforce what his conscience tells him. That is why character is what matters in education. If the doctor – and Hahn is misunderstood here very often – is a fit person, if he is healthy and practices a certain self-discipline etc., he is more likely to ask the right questions. However, if he is a person who has never put himself to the test, also physically badly trained, then it is likely that he will ask the wrong questions. His experience therapy is based on experiences, a certain practice in everyday life. Also in the physical sense. Not that you become a great athlete. But in the sense that you not only practice where you are strong, but also things for which you are poorly gifted or which you do not know at all.

That young people learn about their weaknesses and overcome them to a certain degree. If you are in nature, it is good to go on expeditions, to the mountains for example. That you plan the expeditions. What do we need? What do we take with us? What equipment? Have we looked at the maps? Do we need a compass or just the satnav? Prepare things carefully and conduct the expedition. Two, three, ten days, one month. Then you get a good feeling. You have prepared something. You have been put to the test by doing it. You should also learn to do something with your hands. A craft. Hahn attached great importance to the fact that his students went to a craftsman once a week to make pottery, to do carpentry, etc. to work with their hands. Learn how to create something with your own hands. Develop respect for the craft and the craftsmen.

I think his success was largely due to the fact that he used such simple expressions and images, like the example with the doctor, almost a banal picture. The doctor who stays in bed or who conscientiously asks and then says: alright, I'm coming.

As for the academic aspect, he always said that you should study fewer subjects, but more in depth. Above all, everyone should do a project, regardless of age. In younger years, this could be handicrafts or making a table or producing something with a craftsman. However, something that you really finish to the end. Not something that stays halfway. A finished object. A research project should then be carried out in the last school years. This then became the Extended Essay at the IB (International Baccalaureate).

He himself was fond of the combination of research and travel. He liked to quote the student from Salem who worked on a project in Milan. He had to get to Milan somehow. So he went there by bike: from Salem to Milan. In Milan he had to find accommodation and carry out his project. So don't just sit in the library.

Also group projects. Of course, it was important to have a result in the end. This then became the Extended Essay.

Too bad that the Extended Essay has become much less adventurous in the past ten years. Too many parameters have been set. A lot has been automated and a victim of bureaucracy. It has lost much of its importance and intention.

MG: What was Hahn like – as a person?
DS: He was a very passionate person. When I met him, he was an older person. He worked incredibly hard to start Atlantic College. Everywhere he gave lectures, wrote essays, visited people, welcomed people in his home. He was always, always on the go. Not only because of Atlantic College, but also because of Gordounstoun and because of Salem. Salem was going through a difficult time because of a breakdown at school. There were major internal problems for many years. That worried him very much.

Because Salem was his first school. There were many changes in management. The school seemed to be falling apart somehow.
Very passionate, always on the go and a very good speaker. Really an excellent speaker, always these little stories and aphorisms. You can see that in his correspondence, too. He helped countless people: former students who had problems, people kept coming to him: my son has problems. Can you find him a place in England? He has to learn English. He has not been doing well here at school. Or a Gordonstoun student who had killed someone. And was in prison. Hahn hadn't let him down. He went to see him. He tried to help his mother. Hahn was always there for others. That was his attitude. He liked to talk a lot about the „good Samaritan".
He was born a Jew, then in 1945 converted to the Anglican Church. His family resented that. He claimed that the Jews had missed the great opportunity to follow St. Paul and to convert from Judaism to Christianity. Had they done so, they would have been part of global Christianity. He loved the New Testament, not the Old Testament.
Not that he thought what's in the Old Testament wasn't true. But the Old Testament is a tough chunk. The New Testament is different. It is a new way of life and the turning point is the life of Jesus Christ. There was a well-known historian, Sir Lewis Namier, long dead, also a Jew, an English historian. He takes the same view.

JG: The New Testament is based on faith and grace and not on the merit of one's works and on the Mosaic laws. „Be your own law."
DS: Some older students of Gordonstoun were not very happy with my portrayal of Hahn. They wanted to remember Hahn how they had met him. Of course, they had met him in a very

specific context. As a headmaster, as a helper. Many maintained a close relationship with him after leaving school. They knew: you can always write to him, ask him for help. They knew he was there for them. This is their picture of Hahn. Of course it's justified.

However, one should not hide the fact that Hahn – like many other Germans - was a nationalist in the First World War. He was German and outraged at the idea that Germany should not have any colonies. Hahn was also very ill at 18. He suffered, well, let's say, a heat stroke – it's not quite clear what exactly it was. And from the age of 18 he was no longer allowed to walk in the sun. You had to pull the curtains. Michael Schweitzer – for many years Hahn's private secretary – and a good friend of mine, said that when Hahn traveled, he always traveled with a green curtain around his head.

Even on the plane with this thing. I'm telling this because Scotland was his favourite country. He was already ill when he was studying in Oxford. He was already suffering from this. He was the son of a wealthy family and had money. Whenever possible he went to Scotland. The climate was the right one for him. In 1932 he was in Scotland when the Potempa incident happened: in August 1932 a young man was kicked to death by Nazi yobs. Hitler praised these people. Hahn immediately recognised from as far as Scotland – that was his political radar – this was a crucial moment.

MG: Did Hahn have a family? Was he married?

DS: No, he was not married. The secret of his success is what is called „networking" these days. Many visitors from England came to Salem. He was known in England. After emigrating from Nazi Germany, he started very small in Scotland. In 1934 he found a large building near Veness and opened a school.

MG: What, do you think, can be applied from Hahns' approach today?
DS: Learning to act in accordance with your beliefs. He was very much against drugs. Also against sleeping pills. He was for physical exercise. He was against cynicism. For example, once in New York, when a young woman was attacked and eventually killed on the open street, people watched from the houses in the surrounding square and did not intervene. He wrote a lot about that. That people just stared without doing anything. You can't stay passive, you have to do something. Does the Litten case ring a bell to you? Hans Litten was a Jew and a lawyer. His father had been a Jew before converting to the Lutheran church. His mother was Protestant. He was a lawyer of the defence for communists in the early 1930s. He got the reputation of being a communist himself. He replied: „No, I am not a communist. I am a lawyer. The others are obviously unwilling to defend these communists. So I do this."
Then it happened that Nazi yobs once again beat up someone. Some communists were accused. Litten defended them. And he managed to call Hitler as a witness in court. And he grilled Hitler in the courtroom. Hitler shouted in court and Litten finished him off. It was the only time that Hitler had been called to the witness stand in court. It became crystal clear to everyone that Hitler knew how these Nazi people behaved. And only distanced himself from it in public. But the judge did not dare to continue the trial. He was already afraid of Hitler. That was in 1931.
The night of the Reichstag fire, Litten was thrown into Dachau concentration camp. He committed suicide there in 1938. It is a terrible story.
His father, rector of the University of Koenigsberg, was in a very embarrassing situation: what had his son got to do with the

communists? His mother fought for her son with great courage. She went up to Göring. Hahn knew this and discreetly helped her from England. His brother, sister-in-law, nephew and niece all lived in Berlin. They were all Jews. He had to be careful. He even got together a group that went to Berlin in 1934 to talk to Hitler. They took a memorandum with them. Then Hahn succeeded in persuading a friend, a lord, to write to Hitler about Litten.

In the end, Litten committed suicide. His mother escaped to Switzerland while his father stayed in Königsberg. His mother came to London in 1938 or 1939. Hahn found accommodation for her, gave her money and found a job for her with the BBC. He then found out that she had written a book about all the things she had undertaken – in German. He insisted that the book be published and found someone to translate it into English. And it was printed. Even in America. It was a huge success there. Mrs. Litten went to America and was greeted by Mrs. Roosevelt. All this thanks to Hahn. Hahn acted in a similar way as he did in the Potempa case before. That was very important to him.

JG: Hahn attached great importance to allowing contrary opinions. What happens if this diversity of views no longer exists? If you have little money and have to search for it? If you have to flirt with it? You have little time, even little time to pause, to think, to be critical, to renew yourself. It must be allowed to grapple. Otherwise you get old, you are no longer a pioneer, but you let yourself be determined by time. Time cannot be taken anywhere, but vice versa.

DS: I notice something else. Atlantic College was very often in deep trouble in its early years. Hahn went everywhere: to England, Germany, America. He gave lectures: this is our college. These are our hopes and concerns. He was on the go continuously. He gave

lectures in New York, Freiburg and London within four days. That was of course his thing, his message, his mission. We don't have someone like this these days. We have no one to give lectures on the idea behind the colleges.
We haven't.

JG: If you were to write a book about Kurt Hahn now, what would be the difference to the other books that already exist on Kurt Hahn?
DS: The first difference is that I have all of his personal letters and writings. I am the only one who has them. That's why I have insights that others don't have. That means I would describe his life, with facts. How everything happened. What people he knew, who he worked with. I would give some insight into his letters and documents. Since I knew him personally, I have a certain personal relationship with him. This makes it easier to understand the reactions of others. Both the positive and the negative reactions. I guess I would try to show that certain things he taught are timeless and will survive.

JG: Universal?
DS: Yes. He is criticised for never writing a book. Essays only. In the early years. When he was a student in Oxford. Some essays on education. Theoretical things. Then, when building Salem, a few essays in which he outlined his principles. But during his lifetime he wrote primarily to convince people to support him. Each essay had a purpose: „Please, please support me." He never sat down and explained his educational ideas in a book. That is why some say that he had no such ideas. „He founded schools and raised money – but where is the educational philosophy?"
I am reading his correspondence from 1964. Publishers approached

him several times: „Please write your memoirs". But he was always too busy. „Go there: a lecture here, a lecture there. The day after tomorrow in New York, then Atlantic College: If I don't go there, they won't have any more money. Then everything will break down." At the same time, the so-called „medical commission and accident prevention" was called into being. He had the support of Prince Philip. He had to take advantage of that while Philip was still there for him. He just didn't find the time to write his memoirs. He was also ill all his life. Allergy to light since his early years. Then in the late 1960s he was hit by a car in Scotland and was depressed for a few years. He stayed here in London in his sister-in-law's small apartment and refused to receive anyone at all. „I did everything badly. I just harmed people, I'm dirty". He didn't allow any close contacts there, didn't allow himself to be protected. He then slowly came out of this deep depression, around 1970. However, he could no longer travel. I last saw him in 1972. He could hardly stand on his feet then. He wobbled. He said: „Let's go for a walk." We then walked very slowly for 200 meters and I thought all the time: this big man is about to fall over. In 1952/53 he was completely shattered. At that time he had to leave Gordounstoun.

MG: Breakdown?
DS: Yes breakdown. He was sacked more or less.

MG: Couldn't he work anymore?
DS: No. Depression. He collapsed in 1945, then in 1952 and 1968.

JG: An allergy to light is certainly not an easy thing. In addition, a burnout is obvious if you never regenerate yourself

and don't take a break. So much stress also needs relaxation. Does Hahns educational philosophy only depend on the „persona" or is there something that is independent of it, that is based on a tradition, on a spiritual stream?

DS: Hahn has always described himself as a „midwife". He founded many schools and had great success with it: already in Germany: Salem, Birklehof, Salem branch schools, Luisenlund, the short schools in Germany. In England: Gordounstoun, four or five short schools, „Duke of Edinburgh's Award". Millions of young people went through these foundations. The „Duke of Edinburgh's Award" is now also international. A lot of juvenile offenders went through them, many benefited a lot. These things are going very well. Few people know that they were all created by Hahn. One speaks of the „Duke of Edinburgh's Award" – ah, yes, the Duke of Edinburgh. But it wasn't him who created all that. It was Hahn. He has always worked through others. Of course that was very effective. The midwife has to disappear as soon as the child is born and leave everything to the father and mother.

JG: Whoever takes a back seat as a midwife is of course vulnerable. Just as Hahn never wrote a book himself. Actually a feminine moment. That brings me to Europe. My observation is that Europe has a strong feminine moment. Let's put it this way: if you are not very goal-oriented and do not know: you have to do it this way. Rather, you allow something to develop and you let it arise. Then I think it's a feminine moment. It is very difficult per se. At least pretty vulnerable. We sit together and reflect for a while. We are considering what something could look like. The only thing is that we take the time for it: actually a female moment. Of course not in the gender sense female. A very feminine side.

DS: Yes, yes, yes. Hahn created Salem in the 1920s. As a Jew. Then he came to England in the 1930s as a German. He founded a well-known school as a German. In this sense, he was always an outsider. On the one hand, he knew a lot of people from good families. This is how he exerted his influence. However, it was said a few times: please don't be so active. Be silent. The work you do is important, but people don't like the fact that this work is done by a German. So please take a back seat. He always had to consider that. He was very loyal to Germany during World War II and always said: there are two Germanys: the Nazis, but there are also the others. We have to make a just peace. He had foreseen July 20 exactly. At the beginning of the year, he told the Federal Foreign Office that an assassination attempt was coming closer. The Federal Foreign Office and the secret services themselves were taken by surprise on July 20.

MG: He was awake and quick. You spoke of Hahn's connection with Max von Baden. Max Weber was also in this circle of the Heidelberg Association. Liberal Germany.
DS: Yes, of course, they worked together in the Heidelberg Association, which had been founded by Hahn. Yes, he started everything. Max Weber and Mommsen.

MG: How did he experience the year of change in 1968?
DS: In that year he had lost all energy and couldn't go on.

JG: I can imagine: the generation of the 68ers and he are incompatible. So, I can understand these breakdowns very well. When someone burns for something so much that he burns completely.

MG: He didn't have a family either. Where did he relax? Where did he fill up the tank? Did he workout himself?
DS: In the evening he did his jogging. He claimed to be the world's first jogger. In Green Park. He went from his hotel in Devon Street to Green Park and did his jogging.
I think he was not only the first ghostwriter, but also the first jogger. His success depended very much on his personality. Of his persuasiveness, which he had through his speeches.

And through his phone calls! It was said that he had the highest telephone bill in Scotland. In general: he was always on the phone. A former German minister of culture once said at a conference: Ah, Hahn. Yes, he has the „telephonitis". He was always on the phone.

JG: A pioneer of the mobile phone generation.

Sutcliffe about education / Europe / international schools

JG: On the one hand, private schools and also the theatre festivals advertise with the concept of internationality. You adorn yourself with the fact that people are brought in from everywhere. On the other hand, there is also internationality when it comes to migration. But it is not so popular there.
DS: I have a feeling that the international school system is a business these days.

JG: Does that also mean that this type of school can be transferred everywhere, that there is hardly any regional link?
DS: Yes. These international schools are of course private schools. That is clear. That's why I'm a little sorry for United World Colleges that they are disappearing in this wave. Partly because the United World Colleges only accept scholarship holders. You must have the funds to finance these scholarships. That is not easy. I know that firsthand because of Mostar. It is not easy to raise these funds. For this reason, there is a risk for the United World Colleges that they will increasingly adapt to those international schools. They run a business that may be necessary because the business communities need it, but it's a business.

JG: Doesn't that mean that something gets lost?
DS: I think so. The children who go through these schools also live in a somewhat separate cell, don't they? They have many friends from other countries and speak many languages. These are probably gifted children, because their parents are successful business people, and therefore these children have the best

chances. However, there is a new level of school in the world.

MG: Do these schools also have a special educational approach?
DS: I don't know enough about that. Most do the IB. That is why they have certain educational terms from the IB and have to do certain things, for example community service.
However, it can be done either way, as everyone knows.

JG: Basically this would create another gap.
DS: I can definitely say that.... For a long time I have advocated that the United World Colleges should take over some schools in deprived neighbourhoods and try to set an example there.

JG: For me there's the question: couldn't the idea of the colleges be transferred to certain neighbourhoods in which people live who come from everywhere? It is no longer like in Kurt Hahn's time. Today you have problems with it. That would be really cool.
DS: The problem is that people want to make money with international schools. A good example: there is a school in Hong Kong. If you want to enrol your children – and it's good that you enrol them when they're one year old, it's best to bring $ 50,000 to enrol. You may get it back when the child is 18 and has finished school. Not earlier. As a result, the school has a huge bag full of money, can build and hire people. The money is not a problem.
It's true: Hahn died in 1974 and was ill in his final years, he didn't work anymore. But I think if he lived today he would say: these immigration communities in the big cities, we should do something about that.
What are international schools today? You can find them everywhere. The UWCs are also international schools. That's why I

think a new mission should be developed from the old one. What I think is very important is that a college is part of a national school. This worked in Mostar. The college is located in the building of the former very well-known, large, successful high school in Mostar. If it were up to me, I would try to develop 6-UWC colleges in Eastern Europe within the structures that already exist. So with smaller student units (50-100 students) and integrate them into existing schools in cities, countries which are in critical situations. I would get away completely from the mini-campuses. Cooperation could develop.

That is one side. The other development that I propose would be a foundation of around € 100 million, which would be reserved for countries that are in really bad difficulties: Afghanistan, Iraq, Syria, Eritrea, Ethiopia ... countries where we cannot even think of establishing a college.

We should try to build up communities gradually in these countries – it takes years. The interest of this fund would only be used for these countries. They would be offered to the colleges who would be willing to cover half a scholarship from the fund under the agreement that they would fund the other half. If you had € 100 million, an impossible number, but who knows: 5% interest, i.e. 5,000,000 + 5,000,000 a year, because they would be given to the colleges that contributed the second half, then you would already have 10 million that go to the countries that need it most.

There are definitely other options. You have to get together and think about what to formulate as a new mission. Globalisation has developed rapidly. It has progressed much faster than international education. The fact that there are now so many international schools has nothing to do with any idealistic concept of internationality, but they exist due to globalisation. These international schools are what we call "service schools" in educational science. They supply a service to customers. The United World Colleges should not be service schools, but schools with a mission.

JG: Hahn's educational concept is based on war experience. He experienced wars. He saw how people don't stand by their own confessions. Then he tried to counter this with his kind of educational concept, with his commitment. I live in my time. I think there are few people who show commitment to something. The question is, although there are still many wars, to what extent should the background matrix change? Our time has become extremely complex. Shouldn't this complexity be reflected in an educational concept? What can a concept look like in which war is not the basis? To me, a new way of thinking about this complexity is to say: we live in a world that is coming together more and more closely. This creates more and more fear in people. I feel that there is little preparation for this. This preparation should be rooted in education.

DS: I remember that in 1962 it was of course very significant that the Atlantic College had German students. Those were important things. In the Adriatic College it was significant in the eighties that we had Hungarians, Poles, Russians: people who came from behind the iron curtain. We just had to say that in Rome and we got money. This is no longer enough these days. You can find Poles, Russians everywhere. It has changed completely. In the 1990s, the college in Duino was marked by the Yugoslav civil war. We had students from Slovenia, Croatia, Serbia and refugees from the refugee camps over the years. A boy from Srebrenica who had escaped from Srebrenica and was traumatised by the war and could not speak. That was important. And in Mostar, all you had to do was walk through the city and see the ruins. There is no need to make speeches when the students come to Mostar. You just have to take a walk. The city explains everything. In ten years these ruins will no longer be there. So that you might have to start preaching. This is not necessary at the moment.

I find it difficult to say how international schools, especially the UWCs, can still be groundbreaking. Education is something that should be practiced in every school, no matter where. You have to have a certain concept of education and offer a particular concept of education in this school.

JG: What is education? What should it form in a person?
DS: A very far-reaching question. When you return to Hahn, it means that you learn and absorb something and at the same time develop character traits that encourage you and enable you to put your thoughts into action. This is very important, and Hahn would say: this cannot be achieved exclusively in the classroom. Other aspects must also be taken into account. Hahn was very committed to outskirts schools, he wanted schools that work all day long, that the students arrive at 8 - 8:30 a.m., have lunch together, have activities in the afternoon and only go home in the evening .

He worked very hard for that. During his lifetime without much success. If the full-time schools start to thrive today, this will not be contributed to Hahn – that was one of his basic ideas, which he tried very hard to promote.

JG: A lot has changed within ten years. Globalisation has created an alleged internationality. Apart from that, many

people from different nations are already around. The UWCs did not react to this by saying, as you were saying: either I go to crisis areas and only open schools there because I am, say, a bridge builder. Or I take different approach, where I say: stay here, right here, because here, too, I have to build bridges. Not only in poor countries. Here, yes here. Then this also means: to get together again and again, to evaluate, what is this spirit like?

MG: You know I have been to the college in Freiburg a few times. The impression I got there was that a lot of pre-settings are made, e.g. what something should be like and what you should be like now and in the future. To me this doesn't sound too open. In science when you do research and want to figure out something, you start with observations, questions, hypotheses etc. One thing you never do is determine the result before you start. Neither the result nor the process up to the result are known in advance. That is why you actually do research: You want to find out something that you do not know yet. This in my eyes is the basic idea of openness that you do not know and want to find out. An approach which – by the way – demands quite a bit of courage.

If you create a „should be list" for the UWC student, wouldn't that be demanding patterns for reproduction? Isn't this a kind of branding where the school tries to create „templates" on how to be successful on one side and stay committed on the other? Isn't there much more to Bildung (education)?

For example getting to know who you are in all complexity. Getting into deep contact with yourself and others. Developing an adequate attitude towards life, yourself and others in order to face life in its complexity. Finding your way and a kind of wisdom on it. Being able to protect yourself and others and

at the time to stay vulnerable. Developing a certain level of maturity.
Another thought occurred to me when I read Kurt Hahn about duties, which he considered very important: that you stand up for others. I noticed that there are hardly any more binding obligations: in Germany, both military service and civilian service have been abolished. The duty that one had to perform at a certain age for the country and its society is no longer a liability. I wonder what he said about it?

JG: In Germany there is no longer even a duty to take care of your own parents when they are old and frail. You do it if you feel the need to do it yourself, but as an official tradition it does no longer exist. There is a big social disturbance.

MG: I believe that, on the one hand, the founding idea of the West Atlantic, a NATO school, is no longer particularly attractive as an idea. I also believe that the mission is not reflected thoroughly. The relationship between „inward" and „outward" is not clear enough. Peace has a strong inner dimension. I've always been very interested in this inner process. I applied with a lecture on Gandhi. Peace as an inner spiritual-mental matter. I think there is a limit that has not been tackled. A limit that just makes everything unclear. There are many people who look at the schools from the outside who think: „Well, the scholarship costs € 40,000. Sure, the schools are a nice thing, you can expect something from them. There are some 100 people." I understand if there is a lack of understanding. One link in the chain of communication is missing. That's my impression.

DS: What is the main purpose of international education for you?

MG: Education to openness and multi-perspectivism. Experiencing and discovering that there is more than one view

to everything and becoming able to cope with that. Getting to understand that although there are billions of individuals in the world and hundreds of nations and countless divisions and imbalances, there is just one planet and one humankind. For this I consider it important to put major emphasis on the process of the „inward experience" of the student and the „intertwining" between inward and outward.
This means that in addition to the social, academic and political orientation of the school and its concern to enable an important variety of experiences to the students, intra personal development is emphasised and accompanied.

The students could get the opportunity to learn practises of mindfulness like meditation, martial arts, journaling etc. in which they develop their capacities for dealing with themselves and reflecting on the experiences they are having. One doesn't just look at the youngsters as gifted or even brilliant students but also as normal young people with normal problems and one gets closer to them. Questions like: „Where do I come from? Who am I? Where do I want to go? Who do I want to be?" I would focus on those kinds of questions. A focus that can be expressed through artistic, literary activities, martial arts, meditation and the like. So instead of „change the world" it should rather be „I am the world" and „be the change you want to see in the world".
Then I think that it is important to place a strong emphasis on the connectedness and disruption between school experience and „life after the college". It should be clear that the path of life started years before may be reinforced at school but will definitely continue after it. College is just a phase and a preparation for adult life.

Finally, I consider it quite important that UWC schools are interwoven with the place, the region, country, continent where they are located. In contrast to those international „implants" you find all over the world today. Serial reproductions that serve corporate business, international institutions with gated communities. The contact to the local reality and the region should be strong. Not only an international „caste" should be provided for. I observe that internationalisation creates an international „caste" that is going global. And the communication between this upper class and the locals is insufficient. Often the locals are rather right wing and inclined to populism and the elites are (left-wing or right-wing) liberals. Something is wrong here.

What are the main issues nowadays?

Digitalisation and globalisation now prevail. At the time of Hahn, it was industrialisation and nationalism. We have no answers to that. We do not know. The other day I read: the big problem of politics: a politician always has to know and must be able to give advice. However, there is actually perplexity. You don't know. If you don't know, you just have to find out or invent something. This requires research and pilot projects. You can't solve yesterday's and tomorrow's problems with yesterday's recipes. How does that work? You always find new situations. New solutions are always needed. You can't just go around with a recipe book. A completely different thing, very pragmatic: I think that the schools should also position themselves against these schedules, which currently prevail, everything is pressed into this curriculum vitae. I don't think you can perform well with such a schedule. One could say on

the part of the UWCs: OK. Then come after your national baccalaureate and attend our school for two years. We do not adapt to this schedule because this schedule does not make sense as an external target. The students have become younger than in my time. I think it makes a difference whether 15-16-year-olds or 17-19-year-olds attend a school. At 15-16 you are different from the level of development than at 17-18.
DS: We were the first college to do away with English as a prerequisite.

MG: As far as languages are concerned, the college was a pilot project in my eyes. I still profit from this experience, even today. I believe that a school that receives large amounts of private money must have a pilot project character. Your benefit to society must be visible. Pilot projects are visible when they share their processes and results with others. In Germany in particular, a „separated elite" has a bad image. We could have done a lot more in Duino. When so many teachers come together, so much knowledge, so many nationalities, the environment can benefit enormously.
JG: At the moment we see a lack of the regional aspect in international schools. Before that, the regional aspect was criticised, because the global aspect was missing. Now it's the other way around. It would be important to develop a relationship from one to the other. That the school itself also has a relationship with the other local schools.
DS: We had little influence on the Italian schools. We did a lot of common projects with schools in Trieste, but I think we had only little influence.

JG: Is it really enough for today, if something is based on peace only? In its implication, peace means that there is war. Shouldn't there be another moment? Another base? Hahn also expressed his criticism that no active citizens were brought up in schools, brought up on the basis of democracy. Isn't that still a problem?
Hahn wanted people with strong character when they leave his schools, who develop independent convictions and citizens who stand by them. What was his relationship with Europe like? What is the relationship between UWCs and Europe? Europe currently does not know how and what it wants to be. I see a parallel with UWCs.

DS: Hahn was not a great European. He had a somewhat romantic idea about the whole thing. He often went to America. Especially because of „outward bound". He had very good relations with the American embassy in World War I before the United States went to war. He had certain personal friendships. He raised a lot of money in America for Salem and his schools in Germany.

So Hahn was German, English, American. As for the second point: if you talk to and debate with the board of the United World Colleges, they in no way want to see the movement as a European one. They want the movement as a worldwide organisation. They want people from Africa and Asia. This is meant to be a global issue. That is why Europe is actually not very important as a term. I mean what I feel after yesterday: it is actually important to rethink what the United World Colleges want. What qualities, ambitions and purposes they propose.

JG: The global, international aspect makes too an amorphous impression at the moment. It might have been different 10-15 years ago.

Globalisation now exists and it has been substantially criticised. Globalisation is essentially a capitalist affair. It is not about human dignity and ideas. With Hahn you can still feel that it is about human dignity. And therefore to act bravely. It seems very clear to me that Europe must change direction in the next ten years. Either it breaks down into individual parts or it succeeds in reaching a destination as a common boat. A lot of people want to come to Europe. That is interesting ….
DS: Yes. Why do they want to go to Europe?

JG: They hope for prosperity here, which is obvious, because here – at least theoretically – everyone has a right to it. However, also because there are guaranteed freedom rights. Freedom of expression etc.
How often do Europeans or schools located in Europe think about Europe? About what works and about the problem, but also about the idea and its ideals? And if there is no vision, then there is no orientation. Hence, it is going nowhere. In the meantime, too much has been left to the hands of the EU's business and administrative apparatus. Generally speaking, criticising Europe usually targets the EU. You don't care about what Europe should be? I think a school could be a pioneer in this issue.
How should it be designed to actually accomplish this? Europe is fundamentally different from dictatorial states. Friend and foe, good and bad, right and wrong, values and identity are not determined from the start and from above. Europe is characterised by a project character. As processual and therefore easier to attack. It demands permanent participation from the individual and not just obedience. On the one hand, human rights are enshrined in Europe; on the other hand, it

has colonised almost all regions of the world in its past. The chance would be to meet and reflect, to lift shadows, to be creative. With open results. There is the EU. There is Europe. They are not the same. I think Europe would have to rethink its identity.

And I find Hahn helpful when he says that he is interested in the adolescent. He has something that is important and should be continued and transformed. In my opinion, this is the question of identity that our time inherently carries with it. When you create something big, it sometimes exists independently of the person. Did Kurt Hahn create something that is only linked to his person? Or did he create something that can exist independently of its person? That points beyond his person?

DS: That's a good question. I mean, I think the answer can be positive. Just think of the active citizen. How do you create the active citizen? That would be important in any society: In Moscow, in Istanbul – yes everywhere.

Recommendation:

„Future challenge"
Interesting essay by David B. Sutcliffe published in 2018 in a booklet with the very short and appealing title:
„The International School of Geneva and the United World Colleges in the early years of the International Baccalaureate"
Here Sutcliffes analyses globalization and offers a vision of UWC in our contemporary times.

Pioneers – Marc Glorius

„This film is *paradise*" – Helge Schneider

Pioneers go bravely forward, they anticipate developments, and „are far ahead". Whether in music, business, science, technology, art, politics, society, or religion, some pioneers actively shape development. That can happen, for example, by looking at nature differently, or by establishing unprecedented schools in which students who would otherwise never have met, live and learn together. Inventors, daring artists, universal politicians and researchers, entrepreneurs and civilians can also be such active pioneers.

Most of them are driven by a passionately rooted vision. Authentic concepts arise. In short, they are original individuals who go hand in hand with lifelong training. They transfer ideas into reality, implement and refine them. One can say that pioneers often pursue an idea all their lives. Keeping contact with it, they venture into unknown territory. They give the idea a certain shape. Verbs such as *developing, inventing, going forward, conquering, founding, preparing,* and *discovering* accompany this small group of colorful individuals.

There are also passive pioneers and pioneers of the accidental kind, for example, a German woman from a German city who marries a Turkish man. This was as far back as 1955, when there were only five Turks in Cologne, whereas thousands of mixed marriages in Germany are expected here today. Neither of these two would have dreamed of considering themselves as pioneers, and even more so when you consider that both come from different classes: „ordinary people" and upper class, Kemalist elite and Cologne mock nobility.

The children of these first mixed marriages in post-war Germany – like the two of us who write this book (Jale Maria G. and Marc G.) – were the first in their schools who were connected to two countries, cuisines, cultures and languages within single-family homes. We have a mother tongue and a father language, and once a year or more, we went on long journeys. We went from here to the Basque Country, via Paris, where they damage your car, and from here to Izmir, through the Eastern Bloc, the Balkans, the transit highway. These are pioneers of the accidental kind.

In our noisy times, you'd better be careful with „new" concepts. They are often taken up by different sides and shouted out a million times from all channels, until you are sick and tired of them. They have lost their last bit of meaning. They are worn off. One instantly thinks of „integration" in politics, „art director" (German: Regisseur) in the field of economy, „quality" in education, „authenticity," and „revolution" in the theater and the culture pages of the newspaper.

Therefore, just one last comment on this topic: pioneers are most popular after their death. When dead, they appear less bulky, eccentric or otherwise disturbing. Is it because they announce and design something that hasn't existed yet? Do they disturb the usual routine, a particular interest due to their burning energy? Do they disturb comfortable mediocrity with their explicit radicalism? People like Bach, Beethoven, Hahn or Brandt etc. Pioneers have one foot in paradise, at the roots of being.

David Bruce Sutcliffe (1934-2019)

David Bruce Sutcliffe (DBS): school founder of English origin, principal, teacher. Active in the field of international education, he was one of the most important representatives of the United World College movement and organization throughout his life. He was the immediate successor of Kurt Hahn. He had taught in his school for many years and was later his private secretary. Kurt Hahn in turn (1886-1974): the extremely important German-born educator, school founder and principal. About 60 school foundations are the result of his work, including the Salem Castle Boarding School, Gordonstoun, Outward Bound, and the United World Colleges. When referring to Kurt Hahn, a special term is used: *experiential education*. Sutcliffe managed to incorporate the educational principles developed by Hahn in his work and to ingeniously turn them into reality.

Boarding schools in „strong" places ...

I (Marc G.) would never have dreamed of ever being excited about a school, so much so that I didn't want to leave after graduating (or IB). And yet Sutcliffe was responsible for that with his Collegio del Mondo Unito dell'Adriatico in Duino / Trieste / Italy. A two-year advanced-level college with students from all over the world who prepare their international Baccalaureate on a scholarship basis and live and learn together. The academic program is quite intentionally only a part of the education and training. Life in the community with artistic and physical activities, social service, projects and getting to know the host country completes the program.

In Duino and in the UWCBA in Mostar/Herzegovina/ former Yugoslavia, the other boarding school Sutcliffe founded, the colleges are located in strong places with a very particular character. Their atmospheres are condensed. They almost „breathe" a poetically charismatic power. Both places harbor strong symbols. In Duino there is a castle with an old ruin on limestone rocks with a view of the Adriatic Sea. In Mostar, there is the old bridge that connects the Muslim and Christian parts of the old town: a centuries-old symbol that a peaceful coexistence of population groups with different religious affiliations is possible. The bridge over the Neretva was bombed during the Yugoslav civil war, and quickly rebuilt.

These are locations that speak of war and peace. In Duino, Rainer Maria Rilke wrote his Duino Elegies at Duino Castle. On the other hand, during the First World War, there were terrible raging battles on the nearby river Isonzo, just like the massacres at the end of World War II in the karst region, which begins just behind the Adriatic coastline. For centuries, Mostar embodied the possibility of an encounter between the Orient and the Occident. Then it experienced the terrible Yugoslav civil war with a front line running right through the city.

Those are strong places, in which the elemental forces of nature are present: the singing sun and bare, cragged mountains in Mostar. The Adriatic Sea and the Bora – the irrepressible coastal wind, which pervades everything – in Duino. But these are also places where strong cultural forces work and have worked. Patrician and plebeian culture, pop culture and high culture: simply everything. After all, they are places of multi-ethnic traditions: Slovenians and Italians in Duino; Serbs, Bosnians and Croatians in Mostar. In those places, the issues of border and connection become an experience.

... based on old principles

Kurt Hahn played a key role in the first UWC, the Atlantic College in Wales, which opened its doors in 1962. From the beginning, the UWCs followed a simple and clear idea: education as a peace service. Through the experience of international understanding, selected students and teachers live and learn together according to the holistic principle of Hahn´s educational approach. For the peaceful coexistence of human beings, „seeds" are sown. This was created in the leaden times of a destroyed Europe still significantly under the impression of the massacres of the two world wars and in the cold times of a 20th century with totalitarian regimes and self-destructive thinking. „How can there be peace if we don't know each other? How can we know each other if we don't live with each other?"

Sutcliffe was „on board" from the very start, first as a teacher of German language and literature. He had met Kurt Hahn at Salem boarding school, where he happened to be substitute teacher for a friend. This became a four-year job. Hahn discovered his talent. With the official-sounding title of „private secretary", he then travelled to all of Hahn's schools for a year.
Beside Hahn, Sutcliffe found his mentor in Desmond Hoare, the

brave founding headmaster of Atlantic College. Both were career changers. While Kurt Hahn had made his way to being a school founder and school principal through higher diplomatic service and many years of experience as a political advisor, Desmond Hoare had been a highly decorated admiral of the British Navy in his first profession. The symbiosis of daring, unwavering commitment and the steady hand impressed Sutcliffe. With this steady hand, Hoare guided the school safely through its turbulent first years, which faced a near closedown several times.

Sutcliffe succeeded his mentor as principal in 1969 and stayed in this office until 1982, when he was assigned to build up a new college in Duino / Italy. He was principal there until his retirement in 2002, and in the following years he dedicated himself to founding a college in bombed-out Mostar.

All his life, Sutcliffe persistently and unwaveringly adhered to the basic cause of the UWC: to create and settle international communities, learning and living together where regions had been particularly shaken, destroyed and traumatized by the horrors of war. Here these schools would form a kind of a healing texture for a destroyed social fabric. Here the visionary foundations of a new peace order of the world could be created among the students.

The basic idea that schools should interact with the region, the country in which they are located, means that Sutcliffe's schools are not isolated, remote, self-related campuses. Instead, they are integrated into the localities, i.e. specifically: the school building is in the center of the town. The residences where students and teachers live are spread across the town or city. Students drink their coffee and eat their panini at local bars and restaurants. They walk on the same streets, sit on the same benches, and stop at the same traffic lights. They meet the population. They are part of the population. In Mostar, the college even shares the school building with the local high school.

„Walls are opened "and the campus is freed from the „quasi-incestuous" bad smell that quickly comes up in closed institutions. And what is more, it includes the locals, creates a creative framework that enables relationships. Students are given the opportunity to learn from local people and their culture and to experience it first hand. The school is part of the place and, vice versa, the place becomes part of the school to a certain extent.

Raising the barriers, opening the walls, „décloisonnement"

This „opening of the walls" or „opening up", rendered very precisely in French as „décloisonnement", can actually be found throughout Sutcliffe's schools on various levels. International education broadens national „blinders," through the direct experience of different national and cultural perspectives and horizons and through teaching that deepens this to the shared experience of being in new surroundings that will become a new home. Often this experience of the new surroundings comes up again when, after leaving school, there is an „exodus from paradise" and friends and location disappear in the distance.

Class barriers are softened through the scholarship. It is not the income of the parents that is the criterion of admission, but the aptitude of the student according to merit, potential or need. So you can find a wide variety of students from a wide variety of parents at the college. By choosing the candidates in each of the countries, diversity increases. The often constricting boundaries of families are stretched by living in a community of around 220 students.

But the constricting walls of the classrooms also fall, together with those in your own head. Learning no longer takes place only from books and on the computer. It is not purely intellectual. It takes place through self-movement, self-interest and self-experience; through projects and expeditions; through intense relationships; through close contact to the location; through living together in a multi-ethnic, international-transnational community; through travelling; through an immediate encounter with the culture of the host country in which the college is located; through meeting other people and their culture face to face; through experiencing and dealing with the elementary powers of nature. It takes place through social services and emergency services, through the interaction of all these elements – and through reflecting on them.

Intensa internazionale e mondiale – international understanding

The very particular spirit that magically remains unforgettable to many and that is hardly irretrievable is what makes up the DNA of a college. It is something like its atmospheric substance and boils down to international understanding, what the colleges proclaim as their aim.
The term does not really describe the real experience correctly. „International" sounds like a word without much substance in today's globalized world. The English „understanding" sounds a little superficial and prosaic. German „Völkerverständigung"

(understanding of nations) is too ponderous and French „entente" rather diplomatic. I think the Italian „intesa" best expresses the substrate in Sutcliffe's schools. In „intesa" you can almost hear the word „intense". This is connected to „intendere" (hear, listen, understand). And there is „intesa" in the sense of „agreement". Intesa internazionale e mondiale: These schools make many things possible, even those things one would have considered impossible before. Dream and reality intertwine.

Kurt Hahn

> „*There is more within you*" – Kurt Hahn
> „*Der Mensch kann mehr*"
> A human being is able to do much more – Alexander Kluge

Often there is more potential in a person than you think is possible. There is often more than others make you believe. More power. More talent. A more stable orientation. Kurt Hahn (1886-1974) came from an industrial family, had graduated from high school in Berlin and studied in England and Germany. During the First World War, he worked for the Foreign Office as an England specialist. He later became the most important political advisor to Prince Max von Baden. He was the leading head behind the hapless attempts of the prince to prevent a revolution in Germany – after Willem II escaped – under his reign in 1918.
Hahn later wrote the prince's autobiography and finally he founded Salem boarding school together with Karl Reinhardt with the intention of raising a new German national elite but in an innovative school in Germany. Hahn emphasized that

he had not invented new principles for the school. Rather, he had examined different traditions and brought the best of them together, molding something new out of it. You can find English, ancient Greek, Jewish, Christian, medieval elements as well „reform education" (*reformpädagogische*) approaches current at that time. „It is in education as in medicine: you have to harvest the wisdom of the 1000 years."

After Hitler's seizure of power in 1933, it did not take long for the conservative-liberal Hahn to take sides publicly against him. In 1938, he had to leave Germany. He fled to his adopted home of England. In 1953, he returned to Germany, again as the headmaster of Salem. Several school foundations are his work. If you look at Kurt Hahn in one of the rare film documents, you see a tall man with a pointed nose, whose overall appearance and gestural and linguistic attitude has very little to do with our informal, pop-cultural era. It rather reminds one of General de Gaulle when he explains his educational principles in a rather declamatory style, wearing a grey suit, staring into the camera in exaggerated pathos. However, the content of his words stands in contrast to this old-fashioned, pre-modern posture. He wants to create places where students are educated as individuals with a sense of community. Here they are to discover, set free and develop their own individuality, and learn to assume prudent responsibility in the community.

The adolescents should not be squeezed into „social templates" but should develop their own convictions. And, along with this, develop strength of character to stand up for these convictions in their lives, if necessary, even against prevailing opinions. In the spirit of the reform education movement of the first 20 years of the 20th century, Hahn „focuses on the child". The basis for this is a criticism of the emerging industrial society and its negative effects on young people. From these critical observations, Hahn developed a holistic, community-based model of education that comprises physical, athletic, artisanal, social, self-initiative, aesthetic-artistic aspects as well as trips into the unknown, dealing with nature and political participation. The young people are to be formed in an ideally designed community to develop into mature and active political subjects.

A framework is to be created that enables the students to have profound, elementary experiences that touch them at the core and allow them to have a well-founded self-experience as well as a directive, an inner compass: helping them over the turbulences of adolescence, over the hardships of life and about the determination of race, class, gender and biography.

This high educational aim: the education of political individuals on the basis of ethically rooted personal convictions in combination with a concept of intelligence that comprises much more than mere intellectuality makes Hahn's approach surprisingly modern. One can use Howard Gardner's multiple concept of intelligence or the fashionable concept of „deep learning". The work of this restless, sometimes eccentric patrician is undoubtedly deeply rooted and anchored in the universally enlightened tradition of „the liberation of man from self-inflicted immaturity"(Immanuel Kant).

Although Hahn is one of the eminently important school founders and school reformers of the 20th century, he is not given the recognition that he deserves in view of his outstanding work. His name is known mostly in connection with Salem or experiential education, but on the whole he remains suspect.

There are a number of reasons for this:

- He did not give a theoretical work to „theoretical Germany" but was a practitioner who spoke situationally. And he considered the teaching profession more as applied art than as abstract science.

- *Nur wer allein ist, ist im Geheimnis*: „Only those who are alone are in secret" (Gottfried Benn): despite his enormous network, he was a loner all his life. He was not married. His private life remains private (similar to that of many great pioneers).

- Salem is, so they say, a school for the rich – expensive and exclusive. In general, the promotion of elites is particularly difficult in Germany. Their social acceptance is considerably lower than in France, England or the USA. This fact was exacerbated by Hahn's bourgeois-noble milieu, combined with a conservative-liberal political stance that was completely incompatible with the rising powerful movement of '68. Hahn did not join the controversy of the relationship between the leading classes and the masses. Rather, he more or less completely ignored the fact that modern industrial society developed into a mass society with a mass culture in the 20th century. Since the „masses entered history", the individual could no longer be seen without reference to mass and pop culture.

- Unfortunately, the picture material showing Hahn's premises have an antiquated picture language – especially when it comes to physical exercises or experiences in nature.

In this way, Hahn is difficult to „sell" or control him and profit from him. He definitely doesn't have what it takes to be a pop star.

Sutcliffe: an idiosycratic founder and creative figure

Sutcliffe should not be thought of as a chubby hippie or a hairy '68 type, either. On the contrary: his appearance was conservative: suit, tie, short hair, plus a dynamic appearance and a clear look. He had an aristocratic air.

He grew up on the Channel Island of Guernsey, he, his mother and siblings were evacuated to England before the German troops invaded Guernsey, while his father, a doctor, stayed there. Like many children of his generation, Sutcliffe grew up almost without a father. He later attended Sedbergh Boarding School in Northern England and studied German and French in Cambridge.

Sutcliffe's natural element was the ocean, whether as a „double Islander" (Guernsey and England), lifeguard, excellent sailor or canoeist. In 1976, he crossed the Atlantic as a solo sailor in a regatta. It is no coincidence that the college he founded in Italy is right on the coast.

Many photos primarily show him as a representative of an institution in a management position that is quite conventional. In some photos, however, you might think more of an action hero type: stylish, charming, daredevil.

Indeed, Sutcliffe had an accurate understanding of a situation. He liked public appearances and all his life polished the various roles that he performed: as a speaker with fine British humor, razor-sharp punch lines and a large treasure of quotations and anecdotes. As a „leadership figure" with visions that he conveyed to others insistently and in simple, vivid terms. As a founder and daring doer who went to work with great determination, imagination and rigor. He wonderfully embodied the „Special Ambassador of peace" when he brought together people from different cultures and received and welcomed high-ranking politicians, interested guests and sponsors.

In the village of Duino, they spoke with appreciation and respect of Sutcliffe, the *rettore* who spoke Italian. As a headmaster, he treated his students with strictness and inspired their respect. However, an emotional fire and visionary energy always shimmered through this behavior. As a typical child of his time, he certainly did not reveal his own emotional life or internal and emotional processes. Nevertheless, many of the students felt that he could see their inner value, which touched them deeply. This encouraged them to pursue their own paths.
A crucial and unchangeable aspect for him was the above-mentioned ideal of „intesa internazionale e mondiale" and the con-genial realization of the whole-person universal educational principles of Kurt Hahn.

He worked precisely and developed his ideas with a great attention to detail. The teaching staff that surrounded him was colorful and strong in character. He had a distinctive handwriting and an idiosyncratic handling of his stationery. In Duino, there was a newspaper room with 30 international daily newspapers. His vision was very clear. It finds clear expression in the school life, where Israeli and Palestinian students might be living together in one room, with the intention of deepening international intercultural understanding through meeting, discussing and debating with each other. And through finding expression for one´s own experiences as well as for the perception of others.

The vision was to enable and implement an intercultural peace experience through living together and learning together, so that this experience becomes a guideline in life. How else can the diversity of humanity and its cultures be expressed, if not through languages? Sutcliffe attached great importance to learning the local language Italian besides using the school language English. In addition, there was a teacher for every mother tongue represented at the school, even if it was for only one weekend a month, so that one heard a great variety of languages in the village: they were spoken by the students, but also taught in their literature, their grammar, their culture.

Sutcliffe often found original solutions to transfer and apply his educational principles. It was his concern that the local population and the international student body should have the opportunity to meet. The opportunity to do so was a school trip every year when inaugurating the academic year, with effective advertising. One year it was a trip to Vienna. Without further ado, Sutcliffe invited all the villagers who wanted to join. As a result, the 220-person tour group became twice as large. And nine buses were needed to get all of them to Vienna.

Another opportunity to achieve this connection between local life and student life was in a „residence" (the places where the students slept and lived) in an old building in the middle of the village called the „old offices". The village doctor had a practice on the ground floor. In the hall on the ground floor there was the waiting room, where the sick people sat to be admitted to the doctor. And the students had to go through this waiting room to get to their bedrooms. This led to many – also funny – situations and inevitably to meeting the locals.

Several years had passed since I last saw David Sutcliffe. I had presented our book project by email and asked him if I could do an interview with him. „Let's give it a try" was his answer.

So we met in London Pimlico in Sutcliffe's living room on a mild January day in 2015. January 2015 – that was before the migration crisis with millions of refugees coming from Syria mainly to Germany. That was also before the „rise of populism" with Trump becoming president of the USA. And still one can find these topics foreshadowed in the interview.

Until his retirement in 2002, Sutcliffe was a key player of the UWCs, now his role was not that important anymore. This was not in the least due to the fact that he criticized the politics of the movement. He was convinced that it relied too much on the old success story and was not facing the various challenges of today – for him the only way to keep on going. A few years after his retirement in 2002, Sutcliffe had devised, designed and founded the UWC Mostar, a UWC within a building that houses two local high schools, in the middle of ruins, right on the front line that had run through the city during the civil war. It was in close connection to the place. Close to the places of suffering and pain. The school constantly struggled to raise sufficient funds to continue its existence, little noticed and little supported by other, wealthier schools of the movement.

It was a long conversation, so we returned to our hotel in Wembley late in the evening. Then the next morning a call on my mailbox: Hello, this is David: if you'd like, we can meet for another round of talks. 11:00 a.m. Grosvenor Hotel at Victoria Station. Surprised and delighted, we fought our way through London to the meeting point. A classic English style room: Tea, coffee, sandwiches and off we went on the second round.

The Greece crisis was on the screens in the hall. An end to the EU was being talked about; here, at the latest, I realized how strong those forces hostile to the EU were in England. The evening before we noticed the great number of historical programs that spoke of the past greatness of England. Sutcliffe was very skeptical about whether England would stay in the EU and this was 17 months before the vote. This was only one example of the visionary power Sutcliffe possessed.

In 2015, many things were fundamentally different from 1962, when the first college was founded. The blocks previously sealed off from one another had given way to global networking. The hard communist dictatorships had vanished. Large parts of Europe looked back on a 70-year period without wars. International structures gained more and more weight and importance over national structures.

And yet: this order was not in line with the UWC ideal. A few steps in the right direction may have been taken, many more steps had to follow. It is the idea of the enlightenment that humanity struggles to attain its liberation from self-inflicted immaturity, the ideal of a humanity that lives in harmony with itself and the world. It was shining like a polar star. The school's task was to strive for continual reorientation to actively anticipate social developments. Sutcliffe regarded the schools as the vanguard of a development for the better. Similar to the small high-power pilot boats that safely guide the large cargo ships into port. Small structures that have the ability to anticipate future developments of the world.

It would only be fatal to feed on the fruits of past work and to reproduce the „stencil-like quality" that has already been achieved. Then you would have taken care of today but not of tomorrow and the day after. The privilege and charismatic power vanish if the orientation of the ideal gets lost and there is no strong ingenuous transfer anymore.

Thorough consideration and analysis of the present were absolutely necessary for this.

The situation in 2015 was enormously different to 1960. The issue of the meaning and purpose of the schools was different when the war was no longer immediately present and when there were no more totalitarian dictatorships. Due to globalization, internationality was widespread. A global upper class of expatriates emerged that needed international schools. What distinguished UWC from these „service schools"?

Sutcliffe came from a generation in which it was more natural than today to assume that it was the task of the leadership not only to fill as best as possible the framework of the institutions and organizations they lead as, but to redefine and to renew the frame. And this was to be with a clear view of the current time, with its tasks and requirements. This requires transferring the ideas in a new context. The more genuine and adequate the transfer, the better the job. A real leader was not to meet the target, but also the *Gestalter* (designer, creator, inventor, organiser) of a frame: with regard to the concerns of the organization, the needs of the time, and the perspective for the future. In order to really achieve this, the leader had to include many contexts, had to be of a universal nature and not just a specialist and expert.

For every movement that has been active over a longer period of time (50+ years), the aspects of orientation and recollection are difficult. Nowadays, painful examples can be found in social democracy or the Catholic Church. Times have changed, the movements also contributed to shaping a time and they changed with time. They became institutions, reached their limits, became lazy, rigid, fell apart, or renewed themselves. An appreciation and always daring new transfer of the ideas of the great figures of the movement were necessary. They kept the memory of tradition and origin alive. In „I Sette Messaggeri" by Dino Buzzati, a story we read at school, a prince sets out to explore the limits of his father's kingdom. But the kingdom turns out to be much bigger than expected and travelling takes much longer than expected. In order to keep contact with his point of departure, the prince sends seven of his riders back and forth as messengers between his hometown and the expedition group by using a sophisticated system. But at some point the distance is too far and the messengers cannot come back to the starting point. All that remains now is keeping the memory of the starting point.

Sutcliffe belonged to the generation before the 1968 years. They had experienced the war directly or indirectly in their childhood and were already at work when the student revolution began. They were a threshold generation, often practically grown up without a father in the conservative post-war order determined by necessities, a time in which the immediate seriousness and horror of war, dictatorship and lack of economy can still be felt and sets the course. It was at a time when young men were walking around in a kind of uniform, wearing suits and thick glasses, a time before „Che, blue jeans and Coca-Cola", a time of enormous economic recovery. Europe takes on new contours and nuclear weapons. An iron curtain separates two ideological blocks. It is a time without war. Thirty years of war had raged before, and Europe had finally lost its dominance in the world.

In the men of this generation – the generation of my parents – I observe a common feature: a certain ambiguity: a kind of „on the one hand, on the other". On the one hand: a bourgeois-conservative air, worrying about their subsistence, home, status, and having clear ideas of what decent behavior is and is not. On the other hand: the search for freedom, combined with a kind of boy-scout romance and a deep and far-reaching commitment to something.
In their old age, after retirement, after leaving the official status and power, this „on the other hand" becomes more evident. Deep personal incidents can also contribute to it. Melancholic features, vulnerability, deep motives, surprising originality and radicalism suddenly surface. David Sutcliffe had to witness how his role and memory at the school in Duino was increasingly marginalized and faded away after he left. The school began to stagnate and lost much of the charisma it had gained over the years.

The UWC movement gained importance in number by further school foundations, but in his opinion the pioneering character of the movement was vanishing, overrun by globalization. Sutcliffe had clear ideas about the further development of the school. In his farewell speech he said that there was excellence, but sufficient relevance still had to be achieved. For this, the schools would have to play a „pioneer role in experiential education".

A pioneer embodies a vision. He congenially transfers it into reality and gives it a clear shape. In a speech in 2016, Sutcliffe used the image of small ships that have played a very important role in history to illustrate his school vision: „My amateurish naval studies have led me to believe in the importance of the little ships – the Viking boats that made it to North America and everywhere in Europe, Drake's little ships that sailed round the world and danced around the heavy galleons of the Spanish Armada (…). And I think there is a strong case now for developing UWC along little ship lines, no more expensive campuses, but UWC units of perhaps 50-80 students in each generation, inserted into existing national schools in areas of clear national, ethnic, racial and social tension (…)"

The UWCs claimed to let students participate in an education that was imbued by the spirit of peace and freedom. Students were to find their own way. They were to be encouraged to go their own way. They were to be taught the prerequisites for independent thinking, feeling and acting. Their characters were to be trained. They were to learn from experience. From the experience of an intense, varied, adventurous, fulfilled phase of life. And from reflection, which in turn required time and space for rest, collection and withdrawal. Through in-depth elementary experiences, contact with your own „black box" was to be exposed and strengthened, thus ensuring a basic orientation in life. Sutcliffe firmly believed that through the international school community experience, young people would be so animated and focused that they would carry on this spark in their countries, their work, their communities. This would enable them to act and stand up for a united world through their example.

The students would be like the vines that had saved European wine culture from the raging vine pest (phylloxera) in 1870. Said

vine was immune to the lice and was then used as a day vine on which the other vines were grafted.
In what direction could the UWCs continue to develop so that the issues and the purpose could be realized in a wider scope? How could these schools really become relevant?

1. „Outward experience" is supplemented by „inward experience". It is undoubtedly important to experience a lot, to get involved in many different ways. However, it is just as important to learn from these experiences. A human being makes every experience in his inner self. Hence, it is necessary for the individual to focus on the integration of what someone has experienced, learned and gone through. This can be done by training, self-perception and external perception. Here the focus is on the personal development of the student (and the teacher, too). It is a form of working on oneself.

2. The UWC schools and their headquarters should open up to other movements that go in the same direction. And connect with them if necessary. That is, here too, barriers would have to be lowered and walls torn down. The Anglo-Saxon tradition, in which the UWCs stand, should be widened so that an opening is created that makes room for other traditions: traditions that do not assume an axiom-like separation between subject and object but rather, for example, in which the subject is in the object and the object in the subject, so that one reflects the other.
And traditions in which the intellect is not the sole bearer of intelligence, but that it starts from several centers with an inner connection and is integrated in a larger context. This would tear down the high walls and the „splendid isolation" that intellectualism and the separation of

subject and object in their claim to absoluteness have created. This means joining other big and successful movements from different parts of the world such as, for example, the Isha Institute of Sadhguru or the Presencing Institute of Otto Scharmer.

3. The schools themselves would have to position themselves as a place with diverse relations with their surroundings. The goal would be to grow into cultural and spiritual centers embedded in various contexts.

4. Sutcliffe's idea of the UWCs as a „character forge" for outstanding personalities is in the tradition of the genius idea. This needs to be revised because there are no really all round high-flyers. Every extraordinary talent has its normal sides. Every vineyard, however excellent, has its mediocre locations. Everyone has his or her talents and shortcomings as well as specific „tasks" arising from individual, family, social and national issues. Here it is important to get close enough to the people, to look closely and to pay good attention.

Sutcliffe's ideas also have a heroic tradition. They strive for greatness and heroism. Here, too, it is important to see that minor, everyday things with their repetitions, banalities, and unspectacular trivialities have their justification as well, so that the extraordinary reconciles and merges with the ordinary and the great with the minor. It should be seen as what it is: two aspects of one unit: „You're not a drop in the ocean, you are an entire ocean in one drop" (Romi).

Sutcliffe came a long way. What will his successors be like?

Many thanks to
Dr. *Don* Esser for helping with the translation from German,
Dr. *Doc* Haeusler for helping us with the layout and printing,
Ellen Lewis for a very friendly proof reading and last but not least
Carsten *Icke* Klopfer for some helpful and fairly important
coordination work.